TYPES OF

ULTRALIGHT AIRCRAFT

By Mika Alora

Introduction

The first image that pops into most people's mind when you mention an ultralight aircraft is probably some sort of crude, homemade looking kite like contraption that someone slapped a lawn mower engine on, added a propeller, hit the throttle and yelled "yoo-hoo!" as they blaze down the back pasture in hopes of achieving some resemblance of flight!

I am here to tell you that most modern ultralight aircraft are far from that stereotype. In fact, many modern ultralights or microlights can be quite sophisticated, utilizing state of the art engineering, engines, electronics and materials. There are now even fully electric ultralight aircraft available that can provide up to an hour of amazingly quiet, gas engine free soaring that can be charged with solar panels!

If you have not done so already, be sure to check out my first book in this short read series titled "Learn to Fly on the Cheap...An Introduction to Ultralight Aircraft". There you will find answers to the basic questions most people have when initially exploring inexpensive options to learn how to fly.

This book will dig a little deeper as we explore the different types of ultralight aircraft that exist. All of the types of ultralight aircraft in the pages ahead can be flown in the United States under FAA Part 103. No pilot license required!

Although legally, training is not required to fly any of these types of FAA Part 103 ultralight aircraft, it is *imperative* that you get properly trained on how to safely pilot your flying machine of choice before taking off the ground by yourself. That is, if you value your life! I am not saying that to scare you, as ultralight aircraft are very safe as far as aircraft go. I am just driving home the point that proper training is what will keep you safe and having fun in your ultralight for years to come.

I could harp on the importance of training and safety all day, but we are here to learn about the different types of ultralight aircraft available to you, so let's dive right in!

Powered Fixed-Wing

As I stated in my previous book, one of the most fun and inexpensive ways to get started in powered flight is a fixed-wing ultralight aircraft. These types of ultralights are by far the most common and most popular type of ultralight in the world. Fixed-wing ultralights are simply a scaled down, single seat version of a full sized airplane. They consist of an airframe that is usually made of either aluminum, steel or even titanium tubing, although wood or even state of the art composites such as Kevlar can be found in ultralight airframes.

The wing, tail and control surfaces are usually covered with a strong, light weight fabric such as Dacron. Nearly all powered fixed-wing ultralight aircraft have a three axis control system consisting of the rudder and elevator in the tail and either ailerons or flaperons on the wings. The elevator and ailerons or flaperons are manipulated by the pilot most commonly with a stick coming from the floor of the cockpit or a yoke coming from the dash. The rudder is controlled by foot pedals.

Landing gear can be configured in either tricycle style or conventional style. Tricycle style, which consists of a nose wheel in the front and the main gear to the rear, is the more common and the easier of the two to control on the ground. Conventional style is more commonly known as a tail dragger, where the main gear is forward and a small wheel supports the tail.

In most modern fixed-wing ultralights, the engine is positioned in a pusher configuration, meaning the engine is mounted behind the pilot rather than fixed to the nose of the aircraft. This configuration keeps the propeller wash from constantly hitting the pilot in the face and also helps cut down on the noise from the engine and propeller.

Like nearly all ultralights, fixed-wing ultralights can be built by the owner by plans or a ready to assemble kit from the manufacture. No experience or FAA A&P license necessary! Most manufactures offer detailed instruction and excellent support to help you with your build. Also, many manufactures offer a fully assembled, ready to fly ultralight aircraft from the factory. Just buy and fly!

Another compelling aspect of most ultralight aircraft is their ease of storage and portability. Many fixed-wing ultralights have the ability to fold in the wings. This allows for less space needed to store the aircraft. Ultralights with foldable wings can be stored in a standard sized garage or on/in a trailer. Just imagine taking your ultralight with you on your next camping adventure!

One more thing that makes ultralights so fun is their ability to take off and land in short distances. You do not need a long paved runway or even an airport. A decent grass field with a few hundred feet of open space is all that is needed to safely enjoy flying your ultralight.

Trikes

The second most popular type of ultralight aircraft is commonly referred to as a Trike. Another term used for this type of ultralight is weight-shift. On a trike, the term weight-shift does not refer to the pilot having to shift their weight in the seat, (although literal weight shift ultralights do exist) rather it refers to the way the wing is manipulated for flight control.

Unlike fixed-wing ultralights, which utilize three axis flight controls, a trike is controlled with your arms by pushing, pulling and "shifting" the control bar, which directly controls the angle of the entire wing. There are no ailerons or flaperons on the wing and there is no tail on the aircraft.

The wing is one solid piece usually shaped like a triangle.

These ultralights are referred to as trikes because they almost exclusively utilize a tricycle style landing gear. The engine on a trike is almost always positioned in a pusher configuration on the rear of the aircraft. The airframe is built out of materials similar to a fixed-wing ultralight.

Piloting a trike can be somewhat counter intuitive to a person used to flying with three axis flight controls. When you pull back on the stick or yoke of a fixed-wing aircraft, the elevator on the tail moves up, therefore causing the aircraft to climb. In a trike, it is the opposite. When the pilot pulls back on the control bar, the aircraft descends rather than climbs, as the angle of the entire wing is put in a down position by pulling back on the control bar.

Like most ultralights, this type of aircraft is very safe once you understand their flight characteristics and receive proper training in a trike with a qualified instructor.

Another neat thing about trikes is that they are very transportable and easy to store. The wing folds in and is stored in a sleeve. The wing is easily detached from the airframe, leaving a compact footprint.

Learning to fly a trike can unlock many other doors as far as flying machines go, including hang gliders!

Powered Parachutes and Powered Paragliders

The third most popular type of ultralight aircraft is a powered parachute (PPC) or a powered paraglider (PPG). They are exactly what their names imply; a parachute type wing called a parafoil with a gas or electric motor which provides forward propulsion. They are fairly simple machines, very safe, highly portable and a whole lot of fun!

A PPC is somewhat similar to a fixed-wing or trike in that an engine with a propeller is mounted to a lightweight airframe in a pusher configuration with tricycle style wheeled landing gear and a seat which the pilot rides on.

A PPG is basically the same type of wing, but minus the

airframe. Instead of the engine mounted to an airframe, the engine and propeller is configured on a backpack and worn by the pilot. The landing gear is your legs! This may sound concerning at first, but actually is a non issue as you remember you are flying under a parachute. With proper training, soft landings are the norm.

The primary difference that sets this type of ultralight apart from the others is that the wing is a parafoil and is controlled much like a parachute is controlled, by pulling handles attached to the cords affixed to the wing. This manipulation of the shape of the wing (parafoil) is what steers the aircraft. The engine primarily adjusts speed and altitude.

As mentioned, this type of ultralight aircraft is highly portable and can be transported in the back of a pickup truck to any destination you wish to fly. In the case of a PPG, it will fit in the back of most cars!

Powered parachutes and powered paragliders are one of the least expensive types of aircraft to get in to. They are an inherently safe aircraft when piloted properly. If in the rare occurrence of an engine failure while flying, it is not that big of a deal. You already have a built in parachute! Just simply pick a landing spot and gently float down to the ground.

If the idea of fair weather flying low and slow to relax and enjoy the view sounds appealing, a PPC or PPG may be for you!

Rotorcraft

Allot of people do not think about rotorcraft when they think of ultralight aircraft.

Those people are missing out on an exhilarating way to fly!

The truth is there are several different options available to ultralight flyers when it comes to this type of aircraft. When you hear the word rotorcraft, most people think of a helicopter, but there is another type of rotorcraft often overlooked and under-appreciated called a gyrocopter; but let's start with the ultralight helicopter.

An ultralight helicopter is simply a scaled down, single seat, bare bones rotorcraft. The airframe is typically built out of the same materials most ultralight airframes are made of. The engine is mounted behind the pilot and powers the main overhead rotor and the tail rotor.

Helicopters are a different animal when it comes to the flight controls. A helicopter has four basic flight controls; the cyclic pitch control, the collective pitch control, the throttle and the antitorque controls.

Your "wing" is the main overhead powered rotor. The main rotor is manipulated by the pilot via two different sets of controls. First is a stick between the pilot's legs called the cyclic. The cyclic controls the forward, aft, left and right pitch of the entire rotor head. Another lever located on the left side of the pilot seat is called the collective. The collective controls the pitch of the rotor blade itself. It pitches the rotating blade to an angle of attack to a point where lift is achieved. This, along with the use of the throttle, controls the climb and descend motion of a helicopter. The throttle is also located on, and is part of, the collective. The foot pedals control the antitorque, or yaw, which is compensated by the powered tail rotor.

As you can already tell, flying an ultralight helicopter safely requires a unique skill set that can only be learned through instruction and training from a qualified instructor. That being said, do not let this detour you from considering this unique and extremely fun type of ultralight flying! No runway, no problem! Take off and land vertically, no problem! Fly backward, no problem! Hover in place, no problem! No other type of aircraft offers the versatility of a helicopter.

The second type of ultralight rotorcraft you should

seriously consider is a gyroplane; more commonly referred to as a gyrocopter. This is my personal favorite type of aircraft! If a tricycle geared fixed-wing ultralight and a helicopter had a baby, it would be the gyrocopter.

The unique thing about a gyrocopter is that it allows many of the flight maneuvers of a helicopter and the speed of a fixed-wing ultralight without the inherent pitfalls of either! When I say pitfalls, I am primarily referring to the fact that a gyrocopter cannot stall!

Like a helicopter, a gyrocopter utilizes an overhead rotor blade to generate lift. But unlike a helicopter, the rotor blade on a gyro is not powered by the engine. It is a free spinning, long, narrow rotating wing powered by the air passing through it. As the aircraft accelerates during takeoff, air is forced through the rotor causing it to spin. Once the rotor reaches a certain RPM, it generates enough lift to fly. A gyrocopter is always in autorotation, meaning that as long as sufficient airflow is passing through the rotor blades, the aircraft will not stall.

A gyrocopter has a tail that operates similar to a fixed-wing airplane, minus the elevator. Also, like many modern fixed-wing ultralights, the engine is typically mounted to the airframe in a pusher configuration on a gyro.

Like a helicopter, the cyclic on a gyrocopter manipulates the entire rotor head for climb/descend pitch and left/right turns. Foot pedals control the rudder in the tail to adjust yaw. There is no collective pitch of the rotor blades on a gyrocopter. This allows a pilot familiar with three axis controlled aircraft, like a fixed-wing, to intuitively transition to a gyro with just a little extra training.

Because there is no collective pitch of the rotor blades, ultralight gyrocopters cannot leave the ground vertically like a helicopter and do need room to take off; typically equivalent to that of a fixed-wing ultralight, **but** a gyro only needs about the space of a tennis court to land!

Gyros cannot hover, but they can do a damn good job of imitating a hover. Once airborne and at a sufficient altitude, a gyro does not need forward airspeed to keep the rotor spinning at optimum RPM. Unlike a fixed-wing aircraft, zero airspeed in a gyrocopter simply equals a comfortable vertical descent. In the rare event of an engine failure, a gyro pilot can relax knowing the aircraft will not stall. Simply descend to landing altitude and land.

I highly recommend gyrocopters to anyone interested in flying. They are very safe and extremely fun to fly!

Gliders and Sailplanes

Not every aircraft has to have an engine. For the purest looking for the joy and serenity of silent flight, a glider or sailplane cannot be beat. Liken piloting a glider to fly fishing. It is peaceful, yet technical at the same time.

Like all unpowered aircraft, an ultralight glider can be launched by being towed aloft by another powered aircraft, be pulled by a car or winch or be launched off a hillside by rolling or running down a slope.

Ultralight gliders airframes are very similar to a powered fixed-wing ultralight, with the exception being that modern gliders typically utilize state of the art light weight yet strong materials such as titanium and carbon fiber, although aluminum is common as well.

Gliders typically utilize a stick and pedal three axis control system. The biggest difference between a powered fixed-wing ultralight (minus the engine) and an ultralight glider is the wing. Gliders are designed to, well, glide! The wing of a glider is optimized to reduce drag and generate lift. Because of this, a gliders wing is extremely efficient. To achieve this, the wing tends to be much longer and somewhat narrower than a typical powered fixed-wing aircraft wing. It is not unusual to see a glider with a 40 to 50 foot long wingspan!

A gliders wing is so efficient that upward thermals in the atmosphere can be sought out by the pilot to regain altitude and extend flight times by hours on a good day! Just imagine flying along silently with no engine noise or smell of fuel for as long as the thermals allow. This is but one of the technical aspects of flying gliders. Another big benefit of ultralight gliders is the fact that you do not have a gasoline engine to take care of or worry about!

Electric powered ultralight gliders have become more popular over the last several years with the advent of powerful, efficient electric motors and battery technology. In this case, you do not need a tow vehicle or hill to fly off of in order to enjoy your sailplane. Simply power up the battery powered electric motor, which a folding propeller is attached, take off, reach altitude, then turn the motor off, fold the propeller and glide silently to your heart's content. No thermals, no problem! Open the prop, engage the electric motor and climb back up to altitude to enjoy the experience again.

Ultralight gliders are hoot to fly and are very cost effective to get in to. They are yet another choice you have in the world of ultralights.

Lighter Than Air

    I could not complete this
book without including this
type of ultralight aircraft.
Although these flying machines
are not nearly as prevalent

these days in the world of ultralights, they represent a nostalgic and historical significance in human flight and are available to you as an ultralight pilot.

Lighter than air ultralights consist of hot-air balloons and airships (blimps) as long as they meet the requirements of FAA Part 103.

This type of ultralight aircraft is unlike any of the other ultralights we have discussed. There are no wings, no engines, no landing gear, no control surfaces and no real airframe to speak of. Let's discuss ultralight hot-air balloons first.

There are three types of hot-air balloons. The first is a normal or basket balloon, which is what most of us are familiar with consisting of a basket for the pilot and passengers to ride in which is attached to the balloon (called the envelope) by cords or cables and a propane tank and burner attached to the basket which is used to heat the air in the balloon to provide lift. Larger basket balloons will not fall under the guidelines of FAA Part 103, but some single passenger basket balloons do!

The second type of balloon is called a Hopper balloon. Commonly called a "Cloud-hopper", this one person ultralight consists of a small hot-air balloon and a harness, similar to a parachute harness, for the pilot and a backpack worn tank and burner. The harness swivels 360 degrees to aid the pilot in viewing and with landings.

The third type of hot-air balloon is called a Chariot. This ultralight balloon is nearly the same as a Hopper with the exception of a seat hanging below the balloon for the pilot verses a harness and the tank and burner is mounted to the seat verses a backpack. Like the Hopper, the Chariot seat swivels 360 degrees.

A balloon pilot has to be keenly in tune with the wind and weather to achieve the desired general direction a pilot wishes to travel. Altitude plays a big role in this as wind speed, temperature and wind direction changes as you travel through the atmosphere.

The next type of lighter than air ultralight is even more obscure and less known than the balloon. It is a hot-air airship. Commonly referred to as a blimp, a hot-air ultralight airship is similar to a balloon in that heated air provides the lift. Unlike a balloon, a blimp does not solely rely on the atmospheric conditions to achieve a desired direction.

Ultralight blimps have a small motor and propeller which provides forward thrust. They also have elevators and rudders which provide directional control of the airship. The pilot sits in a seat suspended from the bottom of the airship. The tank and burner are mounted to the frame of the seat.

Airships are one of the most unique ultralights on the planet and sure to turn heads wherever you go! Lighter than air aircraft are very safe and have been around for hundreds of years. They are also light weight, extremely portable and easy to store.

Like all aircraft, learning to fly a lighter than air ultralight requires a special skill set that only a qualified instructor can provide.

If you love flying, do not pass up the opportunity to fly in a lighter than air aircraft if you ever have the chance. Once you do, you may never go back to powered flight again! It is that serine and surreal.

Do yourself a favor and consider lighter than air ultralight flying! If you do, you will become a part of an elite club of ultralight pilots.

Conclusion

I want to thank you for the purchase of this book. Hopefully it gave you some insight and clarity on the types of ultralight aircraft available to you. I look forward to writing more like it in the near future on other fun and exciting hobbies of mine.

If indeed you found this book helpful and worth the read, please take a moment and leave a review on Amazon. Have fun, enjoy life and fly safe!

Mika Alora

Made in the USA
Coppell, TX
08 November 2022

85960308R10029